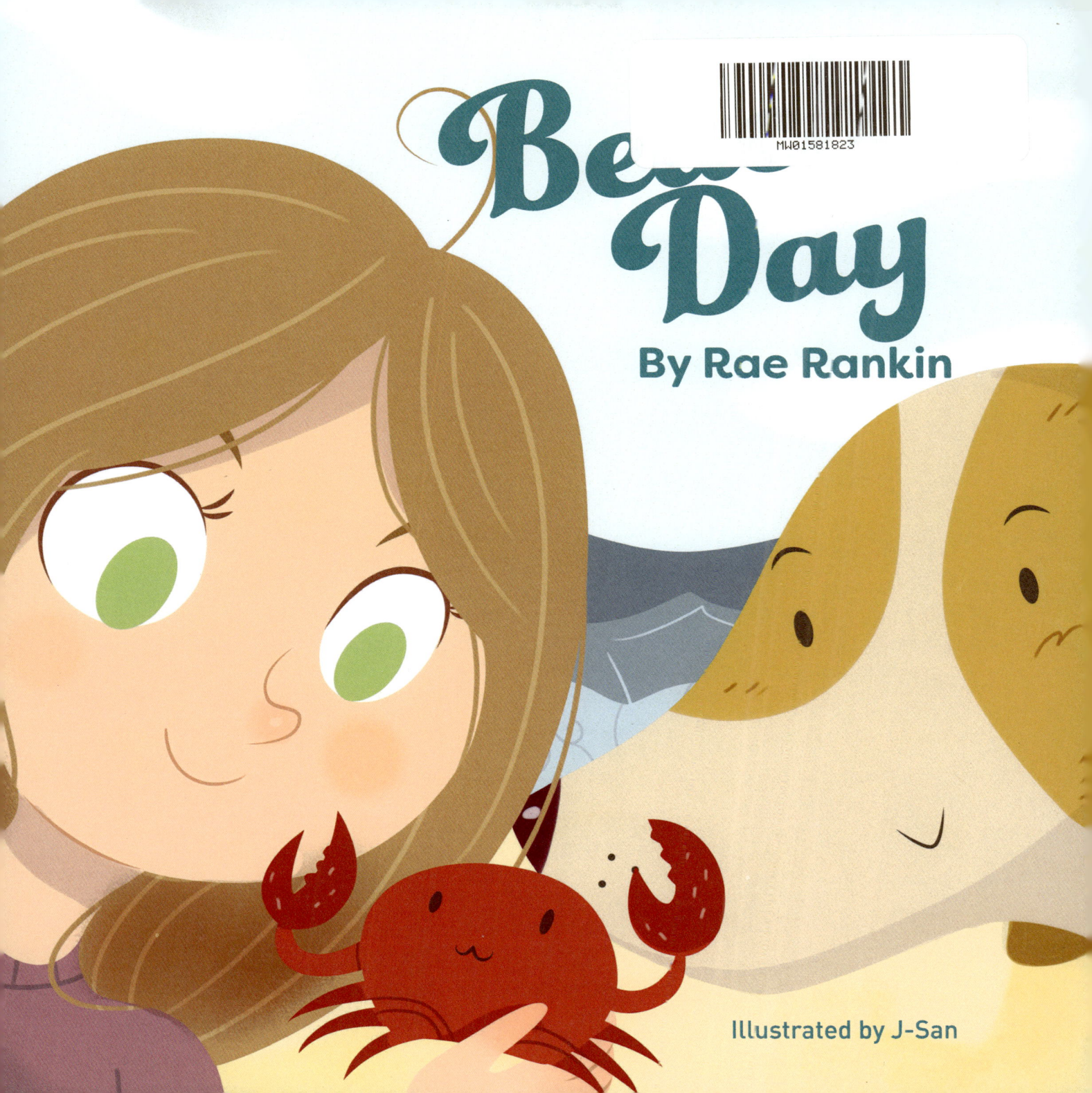

Beach Day
By Rae Rankin

Illustrated by J-San

Text © 2017 Rae Rankin
Illustrations © 2018 J-san Art and Rae Rankin
All rights reserved. Published by Rankin Publishing
No part of this publication may be reproduced, stored in a retrieval system, or transmitted in any form or by any means, electronic, mechanical, photocopying, recording, or otherwise, without permission of the publisher. For information regarding permission, contact raerankinauthor@gmail.com

Rankin, Rae, Beach Day/[Text by] Rae Rankin
[Illustrations by] J-san

ISBN-13: 978-0-9994340-3-1
Ebook: 978-0-9994340-2-4

Typeset in Funkydori and Filson Soft
Book design by Rae Rankin
Editors: Erin McCready and Derek Heinz

For Elizabeth

my Grandma Rae who gave me a love of the beach,
my husband Steve, and my mom and dad.

And for Yachats, Oregon.

*To Nula & Caio
May all your dreams come true.
Rae Rankin*

I've been excited for days; the countdown is done.
Penny barks her excitement; we are ready for fun.
I slip on my flip-flops and race to the door,
Mom and Dad are ready to head to the shore.

We drive up the road and up over the hill,
Past the barn where I ride, all is quiet and still.

Around the next bend, is my first glimpse of the sea,
The beach makes me happy, I am giddy with glee.

We carry our belongings down wooden beach stairs,
Set up our towels and prop up our chairs.
Mom pulls out the sunscreen before I can flee,
Slathers it over my nose, neck, and knees.

I scamper down the beach, Penny right at my heels,
I skip and I dance and do perfect cartwheels.
Beach day is one of my favorite of all,
We've come to this beach since I was small.

I throw my light blue disk far into the air,
Penny leaps to catch it with her own canine flair.
Down the beach she races with her drool soaked prize,
Teasing and taunting and winking her eyes.

We explore pools left from the low tide
In the nooks and crannies, the sea creatures hide.
Over the rocks we scamper to a heart-shaped pool,
It's a gem, a perfect sparkling, turquoise jewel.

Mom searches for shells at the edge of the waves,
She hunts at low tide for those she will save.
"Sand dollars are lucky," she says and holds out her hand,
Three perfect ones lay together, sprinkled with sand.

Limpets and clams, spiral shells too,
In the cool sand, we create a seashell zoo.
A glimmer suddenly catches my eye,
It's an agate, the very first one I spy!

After lunch, we visit a small-town parade,
Settle down by a tree in a small spot of shade.
It's the annual La De Da and anything goes,
The parade has us laughing and stamping our toes.

The afternoon breeze sets my kite flying high,
It soars and dances right up to the sky.
Spirals and dives as it heads toward the ground,
Then dances right up and swirls all around.

Sandcastle building is considered an art,
Mom says I'm off to a great start.
Towers and turrets, and a leaf for a boat,
Penny keeps busy by digging the moat.

We search around rocks for treasures of old,
Mom said that's where pirates have buried the gold.
An X marks the spot where I start to dig,
"Thar' be treasures!" I yell and do a jig.

Dad builds a campfire as the sun starts to sink,
We roast hot dogs 'til they are toasty and pink.
We finish off dinner by making a hot, tasty treat,
S'mores, perfectly brown, sticky, and sweet.

We cuddle under blankets, holding hands to the fire,
Sing songs, sounding every bit like a choir.
I make a wish on the first star I see,
So many things I could wish for, what shall it be?

We ooh and we ahh 'til all is quiet again,
Then clapping erupts faces covered with grins.

We carry our belongings back to the truck,
One last wish on a star for good luck.
It's not very far home, just over the hill,
Past the farm where I ride, all is quiet and still.

I am nearly asleep when we walk in the door,
My eyelids feel heavy; my feet scuff the floor.
Penny and I stumble our way to my bed,
I slip under the covers and pull them snug to my head.

Good night y'all it's been great fun,
Playing all day in the warm beach sun.
I've kicked off my flip flops, I'm hittin' the hay,
For tomorrow brings another fun filled day.

About the Author

Rae is an independent marketing and graphic design consultant transplanted from sunny central California to the wilds of Utah. After two landlocked years (no the Great Salt Lake is not a substitute), her family was transferred to the Pacific Northwest where she can happily see trees out of her office window and where the beach she loves is just a few hours away.

Rae has always had a passion for writing and reading. Beach Day is her second children's book. Her first book, *Cowgirl Lessons*, has been called a book of love and heart.

Rae lives with a loving, supportive husband; pre-teen equestrian daughter; a dog who has her own business cards; and a neurotic cat who eats plastic house plants.

She can be contacted at:
www.raerankin.com
http://www.facebook.com/raerankin

About the Illustrator

J-san is an illustrator and university student from Lima, Perú. He has two webcomics, *Boys and Girls* and *Ravindel*, published in Webtoon and Tapastic. J-san is also the illustrator of *Cowgirl Lessons* by Rae Rankin.

He can be contacted at:
https://www.facebook.com/jsanarte

Made in the USA
Lexington, KY
22 February 2018